BRIGHT

THE UGLY AMERICAN BY BURDICK AND LEDERER

Intelligent Education

IP INFLUENCE PUBLISHERS

Nashville, Tennessee

BRIGHT NOTES: The Ugly American

www.BrightNotes.com

No part of this publication may be used or reproduced in any manner whatsoever without written permission, except in the case of brief quotations in critical articles and reviews. For permissions, contact Influence Publishers http://www.influencepublishers.com.

ISBN: 978-1-645420-44-6 (Paperback)
ISBN: 978-1-645420-45-3 (eBook)

Published in accordance with the U.S. Copyright Office Orphan Works and Mass Digitization report of the register of copyrights, June 2015.

Originally published by Monarch Press.
John Springer White, 1966
2019 Edition published by Influence Publishers.

Interior design by Lapiz Digital Services. Cover Design by Thinkpen Designs.

Printed in the United States of America.

Library of Congress Cataloging-in-Publication Data forthcoming.
Names: Intelligent Education
Title: BRIGHT NOTES: The Ugly American
Subject: STU004000 STUDY AIDS / Book Notes

CONTENTS

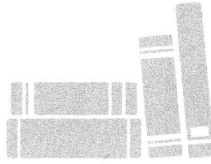

INTRODUCTION TO BURDICK AND LEDERER

. . . .

EUGENE BURDICK

Born in Sheldon, Iowa, Dec. 12, 1918, Eugene Burdick's early life was spent in Los Angeles, where his parents, Jack and Marie Ellerbrock Burdick, established a new home shortly after his birth. Burdick's father died of peritonitis not long after and his mother was remarried to Fritz Gaillard, a cellist in the Los Angeles Philharmonic.

After graduating from Manual Arts High School in Los Angeles in 1936, Burdick entered Sanford University, where he became a psychology major and a member of Phi Beta Kappa. Upon graduating from that college, Burdick joined the Navy, where he served until 1945, rising from Reserve Ensign to Lieutenant Commander. He was awarded a Navy and Marine Corps Medal for action off Guadalcanal.

Burdick began writing in 1944 and had his first publication in 1946, but he resumed his academic career shortly after leaving the Navy. From 1948 to 1950, he did graduate work at Oxford, where he was a Rhodes scholar, and earned a Ph.D. in Philosophy. In the following two years he was an academic consultant at the Naval War College in Newport, R.I. Not until

1957, however, did he begin his affiliation with the University of California, where he became a Professor of Political Theory, and where he remained until his death in 1965. He is survived by his wife, Carol Warren Burdick, two daughters and a son.

WILLIAM LEDERER

Born on March 31, 1912, his parents were William Julius Lederer, a dentist, and Paula Franken Lederer. He and his sister were raised in Ossining, N.Y., and New York City.

After attending De Witt Clinton High School for a year and a half, Lederer worked as a newspaperman for a two-year period, during which time he was a secretary to columnist Heywood Broun, and connected with various New York City papers.

In 1930, Lederer enlisted in the Navy and, after a year and a half in the ranks, entered the United States Naval Academy. A speech defect, stammering, which almost cost him his admission, was so thoroughly conquered that he became President of the Naval Academy Public Speaking Society. Altogether, his naval career lasted twenty-eight years, and included the kind of continuing study which has made him an authority on Asiatic people as contrasted to Asiatic politicians.

Lederer lives in Honolulu with his wife, the former Ethel Victoria Hackett, and three sons.

THE UGLY AMERICAN

HISTORICAL BACKGROUND

INTRODUCTION

The stage for *The Ugly American* has been set for a thousand years, if we are to believe the boast of the Viet Minh, first serious backers of democratic nationalism in Viet Nam. Actually, the earliest date which concerns us is 1858, when French colonial rule began in that part of southeastern Asia known for so long as Indochina. Far more immediate, however, are the years of World War II and, especially, the ones since the end of that conflict. For it was then that the spirit of democratic nationalism developed, and was carried on in war and peace until today. In the light of modern alliances, serious recognition must be given to that far earlier period, however. The thousand years of which the Viet Minh bragged were years of resistance to Chinese invasion and exploitation. It has left a feeling toward China which cannot be totally disregarded despite the lines of alliance along which the battle rages today.

The first roles played upon this stage were the rival ones of French colonialism and native nationalism. As we watch today, two other players, International Communism and American Intervention, both possessing potential for nuclear war, play out more sinister roles.

FRENCH COLONIALISM

The story of France in Southeastern Asia is much the same as that of colonialism in other parts of the world. There are the usual citations by the mother country of how well the white man's burden has been carried in the fields of health, sanitation, and agriculture. These, in turn, are countered by native accusations of exploitation, tyranny, and humiliation which followed the original invasion. There is time here only for a brief analysis of the manner in which colonialism has contributed to the background of *The Ugly American*. One undeniable result is that colonialism has become an immediate cause of distrust, distrust which has made colonialism's offers of national recognition seem too small and too belated a gift to some and has seemed to others to provide a rallying ground for Communism. Unfortunately, even the briefest resume of colonialism in Viet Nam seems to justify the prevalent native attitude.

From the first day, confidence and colonialism did not go together in Viet Nam. One cannot help drawing this conclusion from a description of the French arrival found in The Struggle for Indochina. There the author, Ellen J. Hammer, describes the hypocrisy surrounding that event by reprinting a letter written so early as 1862 by Captain Gosselin, a French officer in the Franco-Spanish expedition sent to Viet Nam in 1858. Gosselin wrote "Our compatriots, not well informed on history, suppose that France came to... Annam solely for the protection of missionaries... The missionaries, in reality, have only been the pretext... The loss of India...imposed on us the obligation to set foot in the China seas, the only alternative being our falling into a state of contemptible inferiority..."

This original hypocrisy revealed itself close to a century later in French offers of nationalism to Vietnamese. After years of uninterrupted rule in a colony where the major source of wealth was rubber, Vichy France found itself unable to stamp out the rising nationalism fostered by the Viet Minh. Although left alone in that part of Asia during those war years by the real rulers, the Japanese military, France's own forces were weak, and they had to counter the Viet Minh with a proposed Federal Council of Indochina. This, however, was actually an offer of partnership extended to the native elite only. Even they were treated distinctly as second class citizens and not admitted to positions of real political or economic power. This policy not only continued but increased in intensity after Allied victory and the unauthorized support of French colonialism by the British. To it can be credited the failure of a later attempt to oppose Ho Chi Minh's Democratic Republic with an Associated State headed by the former emperor, Bao Dai. This failure was followed by the Indochina War.

NATIONALISM

Originally, nationalism in Viet Nam took a monarchial form. A monarchy dependent, in theory, upon the people. In his religious role, the Emperor was absolutely supreme but could forfeit this authority by abusing his power. Once stripped of his heavenly mandate, he could legally be an object of rebellion. This phase of Vietnamese nationalism is not important to understanding Lederer's and Burdick's story save on one point. In both Hammer's The Struggle for Indochina and Vo Nguyen Giap's People's War, People's Army, the village character of Viet Nam's nationalism is stressed. Historically, the Vietnamese have always identified themselves with their particular village rather than with their central government. They still do so today, and the significance of this characteristic allegiance will be discussed more fully in another section of this background, Guerrilla Warfare.

For the purpose of understanding *The Ugly American*, discussion of nationalism may be limited here to the two opposing forms which have appeared in Viet Nam in recent years, particularly between the end of World War II and the final French defeat in Indochina.

One was the Democratic Republic of Viet Nam, headed by Ho Chi Minh, and backed by the Viet Minh. The other was a federation proposed by the French, and headed by the former emperor Bao Dai.

The Viet Minh were at first independent, but finally associated openly with Communism. It was they who, under the leadership of General Vo Nguyen Giap, defeated the French at Dien Bien Phu, and ended the war in Indochina.

Undoubtedly hurt internationally by their identification with Communism, the Viet Minh nevertheless were the only group to draft a republican constitution. Their goal was always true nationalism; they never wanted to remain a colonial assembly. Perhaps the strongest proof of their democratic objectives lies in the intensity of their opposition by the French. The Viet Minh were described by the French in terms of "terrorism" "Communism," and "totalitarianism." They were attacked by the French on the battlefield and in politics. The political opposition gave rise to the second and weaker form of nationalism described earlier, a federation of Indochinese states known first as the Indochinese Federation and later as the Associated State. The French selected Bao Dai as head of this organization, and as a suitable rival for Ho Chi Minh.

They were no more successful in this counter diplomacy than they were later in battle. Although Ho Chi Minh's prestige was undoubtedly hurt by his identification with Communism, that of Bao Dai was even more damaged by his association with French colonialism. Vietnamese everywhere could not help noticing that Communists made no discrimination based upon race. They also had learned during the last one hundred years that liberty, equality and fraternity were distinctly not French exports.

Indeed, this French-sponsored nationalism proved to be, in some cases, more of a boomerang than a counterattack. Sponsored youth movements under the Federation became hotbeds of the kind of nationalism not desired by the French. Also Vietnamese, employed for the first time at equal wages for equal work, later proved valuable trained servants for the Democratic Republic. Still another cause of failure was its inherent quality of contradiction. What the Colonials gave with one hand, they took back with the other. The same middle and upper class natives who were apparently conciliated were still barred from any real political or economic power. The majority of Vietnamese chose Ho Chi Minh - but war followed.

The unfortunate fact that Viet Nam alone had to attain nationalism by means of war is discussed by Hammer in The Struggle For Indochina. After reminding us that various forms of nationalism were acquired peacefully in such neighboring areas as Burma, Indonesia, the Philippines, India and Pakistan, the author gives the following reasons for Vietnamese exception. In her opinion, they were first, a French failure to recognize the strength of nationalism and hence a subsequent failure to deal with it realistically. Second, she attributes war in this area to Communist domination of nationalism, which cost the latter the international approval that might have prevented conflict.

An attempt has been made here to show how colonialism bred mistrust, and how nationalism had its main roots in isolated villages. The mistrust and the country mentality are constantly mentioned without clear explanation in *The Ugly American*. A summary of International Communism, American Intervention, and Guerrilla Warfare may also help in understanding the background of this story.

INTERNATIONAL COMMUNISM

This particular offspring of Marxism constitutes, in Hammer's opinion, the gravest menace to American independence which our country has ever experienced. It is doubly dangerous to the extent that it compels us to let Russia dominate situations abroad. Whenever its threat arises, we abandon thought of everything else, and let it influence our foreign policy completely. Thus our actions abroad can be controlled almost as much by Moscow as by Washington. Our task is made increasingly difficult by our commitment to defend not only ourselves, but others, against its aggression.

Some of the initial advantages of International Communism in this contest are discussed by Roger Hilsman in his Foreword to Vo Nguyen Giap's People's War, People's Army. Communists can sponsor internal war within another country, while we have to wait until a situation becomes uncontrollable. They can be destructive where we try to construct, and they can exploit misery where we are obligated to cure. In all these cases they can move not only first but infinitely more swiftly than we.

Still another reason for Communist success is put forth by C. Northcote Parkinson in East and West. There, the author's words are ominously reminiscent of Deong in *The Ugly American*.

Quoting Michael Edwards, Parkinson writes, "The failure of the West in Asia...was a failure of inspiration. The West had no clear cut faith to offer those it ruled because it had none that it really believed in itself."

Be that as it may, Communism was welcomed from the beginning in southeastern Asia. Also it is not only openly but gratefully recognized by the Ho Chi Minh regime today. A Viet Minh radio declared, on the occasion of their new country's fifth anniversary, that without the Communist Party there would never have been a Democratic Republic of Viet Nam.

Probably the greatest reason for Communist success was the keeping secret of their ultimate goal. Communism was popular with the Viet Minh because, in their minds, it made no racial discrimination, was hostile to the French, and apparently had no wish to enslave people. But the chief architect of its success, Ho Chi Minh, was careful to withhold the second plank in his two-fold scheme for nationalism. The first, winning independence under a bourgeois-democratic government, was proclaimed everywhere. The second, a later proletarian revolution, was never mentioned, because Ho wisely decided that the Indochinese were not ready for it.

AMERICAN INTERVENTION

The policy of American Intervention in southeastern Asia has two basic causes. The first is our determination to contain International Communism. Second, we soon find ourselves compelled to protect the enormous investments made as a result of this original determination. Also, too often, we are faced with an embarrassing question. Committed to support self-determination by Asians, we frequently find ourselves wondering whether we must protect them from their own determination, should it be pro-Communist.

As Rupert Emerson writes in the Preface to E. J. Hammer's *The Struggle for Indochina*, "The United States, as a champion of the rights of peoples to self-determination, backs the claim of the Vietnamese to make their own free choice in the world; but if they should choose Communism, as seems not unlikely, is it then also the American obligation to save them from themselves?"

The result, again, in Emerson's words, has been a "...new American doctrine of 'massive retaliatory power' to be applied at places and within means of our own choosing...." Coupled to this was a theory that war was least likely if all doubts as to our willingness to use this power were dispelled. Our enormous expenditures in the Indochina war made southeastern Asia the place of our choosing, and only removal of any doubts in the mind of Red China may stand in the way of an unleashing of massive retaliatory power.

GUERRILLA WARFARE

In Viet Nam only two kinds of successful war are possible. One is nuclear, which no country dares to wage. The other is guerrilla, where the prize is the village, just as it was a thousand years ago.

This was the type of fighting employed by Vo Nguyen Giap to beat the French in Indochina. It is not a positional warfare with fixed political boundaries; and victory, not territory, is the object of the guerrillas. Although adept at this warfare of night attacks and terrorist assassinations, Giap was not its originator. He borrowed his ideas from Mao Tse-tung, although politics kept him from admitting this. Nor was it used for the first time by that leader of Red China. American colonials waged guerrilla warfare against the British, Spaniards employed it against Napoleon, and the French found it a valuable weapon against Germans in the Franco-Prussian War. Always it was most effective in isolated communities and at times when regular enemy armies were fighting elsewhere.

Giap's own formula for successful guerrilla war is restated for us by Roger Hilsman in his foreword to that young Communist general's work, People's War, People's Army. It is three-fold. First, the enemy's power advantage must be reduced by many small victories. Second is that stage in which guerrillas shift from defensive war to fighting on even terms, and finally to counteroffensive. Third is a final shift from pure guerrilla fighting, to mobile war without battle lines, to a combination of mobile and positional war.

Hilsman also points out that Americans cannot permit themselves to match some of the more brutal aspects of this type of war. Yet neither can they cope with it unless they understand some of the principles upon which it is based. First, guerrillas can operate successfully in hostile communities. An anti-Communist majority is no reason for feeling safe. Hilsman draws the analogy here of the Chicago small-businessman who drew small comfort from the knowledge that most Chicagoans were not pro-Capone, while he was being victimized by racketeers.

Second, politics always travels with guerrilla warfare. Motivation in Communist guerrillas is high to the point of fanaticism. They must be countered with equal motivation or opposition will fail.

Third, the objects of guerrilla attack, namely the villages, must be made safe. The barbed-wire-encircled village must replace the stockades of our own early settlements, as they replaced the feudal castle of medieval times. Now as then, the curfew must be enforced, even under penalty of death. Naturally, no one likes to feel that his right to stay out after sundown can be taken away from him. However, the deadliness of guerrilla warfare demands that anyone moving outside the protected village after dark be treated instantly as an enemy.

Finally, we must be aware at all times of the difference between guerrilla and traditional war. So different is it that we can win only if we fight fire with fire, and match guerrilla attacks with guerrilla methods. Heavy equipment is useless, and even planes are of little assistance. Helicopters are more helpful, but guerrillas can be completely beaten only by foot soldiers fighting on their own ground.

No attempt has been or could be made here to cover the background of the struggle in southeastern Asia. Instead, an effort has been made to describe the setting against which Finian and Atkins had to overcome suspicion. And against which Deong was transformed, and Wolchek and Monet experienced apparently inexplicable defeat. These things, together with Finian's final success when Communism was exposed as Nationalism's foe, may be more easily understood when considered in the setting in which the events took place.

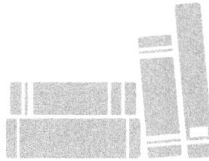

THE UGLY AMERICAN

CHAPTER ONE

· ·

LUCKY, LUCKY LOU #1

In fictitious Sarkhan, United States Ambassador Louis Sears suspects he is being caricatured by a leading Sarkhanese newspaper but can't be sure. Marking time here until his real political reward, a federal judgeship, comes through, Sears can't speak the language of the country he is supposed to be influencing. News comes that an American, John Colvin, has been beaten unconscious. Characteristically, Sears accepts a rumor that Colvin was molesting native women, but the truth is far different.

A former OSS agent in Sarkhan, Colvin has returned to help the people. He is preparing powdered milk, when Deong, his former devoted native friend and ally during OSS days, and now a Communist, appears. Deong, by a trick, convinces the native women that Colvin was going to put an aphrodisiac in the milk.

Afraid of losing a probable American loan, the newspaper publishes a flattering editorial. The Ambassador is pleased, but still Colvin will be sent home.

Comment: This book is an angry novel with a deadly warning. Yet its authors never fall into the trap always open to writers with a message. They think in terms of story and action, not in a series of lectures. Their novel may intend to reform, but it is excellent entertainment, and few readers will put it down. Slashing, blunt, and hard hitting, it is a bombshell.

If you can't communicate, you cannot influence, and ambassadors are supposed to influence. These truths are self-evident everywhere, apparently, save in the United States Foreign Service. We are reminded of them in the opening chapter of this story. But we see this particular example of stupidity in foreign policy only if we are interested in the predicament of a fat man. Will he ever be able to understand how he has been insulted by a cartoon if he cannot read the language of the country in which he represents the United States?

The art of presenting ideas through narration is everywhere exhibited in this chapter. The importance of communication to influence, for example, is shown and not spelled out. So, too, is another American diplomatic failure, equally serious in the minds of the authors. This is the placing of mediocre men where talent is needed. That the State Department so fills its embassy staffs is a fact conveyed to the reader long before it is specifically expressed. We do not need to wait for Deong's reference to "clerks" and Prince Ngong's use of the word "stupid." The point has already

been made by Sears' political-plum appointment to a post he didn't want in a country he couldn't locate.

Other features of fine writing are seen in this chapter. One is inference made almost inevitable by contrast. The other is shock or emotion produced by detailed description. These authors believe that lack of communication is a tragic flaw in our foreign policy. Yet ignorance of language is not the only barrier to communication. Too wide a gap is placed between the Embassy and the natives. The beautifully maintained embassy grounds end in a wrought iron fence. An even higher fence lies between its inhabitants and those women plodding to market outside, as their ancestors did thousands of years ago. There is not enough understanding on one side, not enough acceptance on the other. And so far we see no attempt made to vault the fence.

Certainly an example of realism, this book evokes vivid pictures in its detailed descriptions. The authors show a clinical observation of life as they describe the actions of their characters. But theirs is not the unselective zeal of a Theodore Dreiser which drives them to report everything they observe. And certainly they are not guilty of determinism which takes all choice away from the characters. The faults here "lie not in the stars" but in the United States Foreign Service, especially when it comes to appointments.

Their use of detailed description, though vivid, is comparatively infrequent. It is not used everywhere, but only to increase the savagery of a few scenes. The bullet blowing out the monk's brains, and the pin driven twice through Colvin's flesh are examples of this.

THE UGLY AMERICAN

CHAPTER TWO

. . . .

LUCKY, LUCKY LOU #2

The Russian Ambassador to Sarkhan, Louis Krupitzyn, is a marked contrast to Sears. His life is devoted to the diplomatic service. In preparation for this particular post, he has studied Sarkhanese diet, ballet and music, and Buddhism.

In Sarkhan he first cements alliances and then turns his attention to the enemy. Taking advantage of official America's ignorance of Sarkhanese, he steals credit for American generosity in time of famine. Thousands of bags of free rice arriving from America are labeled by his agents as gifts from Russia - and none of the Americans present can read the label.

In a letter from Krupitzyn to Moscow, he asks for information about a Catholic priest, Father Finian, working as an agitator in Burma.

Comment: Is it a novel? If so, where is the hero? The reader will ask this many times as he continues. But the question will first arise in Chapter Two. The abrupt change in scene will not necessarily bring it about, for the novelist's canvas is a broad one, and accommodates many characters. Neither will the introduction of a new story, for again the novel affords its author room for subplots. And presumably Louis Krupitzyn could have been introduced merely to accentuate Sears' stupidity, if a wise man can be a foil for a fool. Yet the second chapter sets a seal of finality upon the first which makes us doubt whether either are subordinate to anything. Chapter One ends with Colvin hanging over the proverbial cliff. Will he plummet back into the obscurity of Wisconsin? Or will he climb up to renew his one-man campaign against Communism, with a different kind of eye out for Deong? His name does not appear in Chapter Two, and we begin to wonder about the word, "novel." Were we to know that we would never again see the name Krupitzyn, our confusion would increase.

There are reasons for wonder. People who should know contradict each other on the nature of this book. The Chicago Sunday Tribune referred to it as an "angry novel." Conversely, Richard F. Shepherd, writing in the New York Times, December 4, 1965, calls it a series of short stores. If the latter, at least most of them possess the same theme, and one worthy of a novel. It is the impact of official American mediocrity, stupidity, and arrogant insularism upon a sensitive Asiatic nature in areas marked by lack of education, capital, and industry. If we accept this as a theme, then perhaps the hero is actually the homely engineer who bears that title, but who appears in only two chapters and is mentioned only in two others.

Be that as it may, Chapter Two shows us both authors as masters of narrative writing techniques, whether they be scene, summary or description. The art of condensation illustrated in the second, for example, even affords an argument for the "short story" theory of this book. In one seven-line paragraph Louis is transformed from a child witnessing his parents' murder to an adolescent hating the group they represented. And the killing itself might have been a scene represented within a picture frame. In another way, however, the writers swing back toward their role of angry novelists with a message. They again employ contrast and action to stress America's dangerous incompetence in foreign affairs. Nor does the chapter leave us with the final single impression of Krupitzyn's ability, as a short story should. Instead, we wonder about Father Finian. How will Louis fare against a foe he respects as much as he gleefully despises Sears?

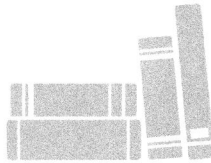

THE UGLY AMERICAN

CHAPTER THREE

. . . .

NINE FRIENDS

An encounter as Navy chaplain with a fanatically communist American Marine drove Father Finian to study Lenin and his disciples. Now he welcomes a Jesuit assignment to Burma which will give him an opportunity to combat what he regards as another example of the occasional diabolical testing of men's souls. He learns to speak Burmese, suffers the agonies of dysentery, finds disciples among the Burmese, and overcomes native suspicions of the white man.

He publishes a native paper in which he reprints written statements of contempt and cruelty toward peasants, authored by leading Communists. Attempts by Communists to suppress the paper are futile, as is their effort to keep secret from Finian the arrival of their star troubleshooter, Vinich, whom Father Finian exposes.

Comment: The charge of Deong is refuted in this chapter. Some Americans do know the power of an idea. The tragedy lies, these authors imply, in the fact that only unofficial Americans recognize this. Forgotten by officials in the Far East are those concepts of freedom and dignity forged for America in her own revolutionary war. Father Finian wins not merely because he discerns in the enemy the ability to use the powerful techniques of his own organization. Nor is his victory based solely upon a dedication to preparation matching and even surpassing that of Krupitzyn. He is triumphant here mainly because of his faith in men. He believes they will detect flaws behind the most plausible fronts if they are guided subtly, not pushed violently, toward such detection. Indirect help through questioning by a fellow learner was welcome to the Sarkhanese. Authoritative denunciation of Communism from on high by a Western white man would not have been.

Part of the message of this book is spelled out again in this chapter for United States officials to read. If you wish to influence foreign people, pay them the compliment of learning their language. Don't antagonize them by making them speak yours in a land where you are the visitor. If you wish to know them, adopt their way of life regardless of the cost. You can be one with them at a meal in their own quarters, but never in an American commissary or a PX. Above all, treat them with dignity. Let them share in the help you give, instead of making it cost them their self-respect. In this chapter we see another reaction to Communism and its influence. American official ignorance sees it as something to be "bought off." To life-hardened and observant Deong as to the child, Louis Krupitzyn, Communism is the hand grasping the revolver. To the adult Louis and to the young marine in the Russell Islands it was a cause whose ends could justify every crime; a cause for which they would die, and carry with them into death their unshakable convictions. To Father Finian, it was the face of the devil. Hence the priest did not fall into the error committed by John Colvin. To Colvin, Communism was a mirage luring on temporarily sick friends, which would disappear as soon as they were made economically well. It could be ignored by the healthy physician as he worked on the cure. Or so he thought, until one of its disciples appeared with a gun.

Finian makes no such mistake. Instantly he recognizes it as a deadly foe which must be attacked immediately in the war for men's souls. Bribes, prizes, even real economic independence, will not be enough. First, a few men must become convinced that there are certain things they want. Then they must want them with a zeal unsurpassed by any other group of men. Finally, they must come to realize that these things will never be attained under a Communist majority. Such a nucleus, so armed, will be able to exploit contradictions in the specious arguments of Communism.

THE UGLY AMERICAN

CHAPTER FOUR

EVERYBODY LOVES JOE BING

Joe Bing, considered one of the State Department's most popular figures, is described in less flattering terms by visiting Setkya newspaperwoman Ruth Jyoti. She characterizes him as loud, tactless and snobbish. She is equally critical of the San Francisco Press and insular Americans in Asia who speak only English.

She does mention an exception, however. This is Bob Maile who, with his entire family, plunged himself into Asiatic life as completely as he could. The result was that through his influence a false story was checked out and killed. If printed, it could have severely injured the American cause.

Comment: Their descriptive powers save the authors from becoming propagandists with a message in this chapter. Ruth's notes read not like her personal observations, but a reiteration of the writers' now familiar theme. Still, we can see her writing them. Also, through her, Joe Bing and Bob Maile come alive. They capture our interest, and become better carriers of the book's message than Ruth, with her carefully worded statements.

THE UGLY AMERICAN

CHAPTER FIVE

· ·

CONFIDENTIAL AND PERSONAL

In a private letter to his friend Dexter Peterson, in the State Department, Ambassador Sears is unconsciously amusing. His proud assertion that he has never seen a native Communist at a social function or an official dinner is classic. He cites the Eastern Star's compulsory about-face editorial as proof of his popularity. His letter calls Colvin and Finian crackpots, and he is firmly convinced that a hundred thousand handbills, telling the true story of the rice delivery, have completely wiped out the damage dealt by Krupitzyn. He closes his letter with an appeal for pretty girl secretaries, and for Joe Bing.

Comment: Louis Sears brings us the angry message of this book much more clearly by inference than does Ruth Jyoti in her direct criticisms. The dangerous qualities of mediocrity and incompetence

reveal themselves in every line of his letter. Even more clearly do we see the truly deadly one of clownishness. If Russia could not stand ridicule in Northern Burma, neither can the United States in Sarkhan. Sears is truly a fit subject for a cartoon.

THE UGLY AMERICAN

CHAPTER SIX

. . . .

EMPLOYMENT OPPORTUNITIES ABROAD

In a speech to applicants for jobs in the United States Foreign Service. Joe Bing is easy and friendly. His role is that of a confider on the inside giving the lowdown not advertised to everybody. He stresses the high standard of living at low cost and the attractive life. Among the accepted applicants are Marie MacIntosh, a Pentagon stenographer, and Homer Atkins, a retired engineer.

Comment: For the first time there is continuity between two successive chapters in this book. Sears' letter in the preceding chapter is being answered in this one. He has written to Washington for pretty girl secretaries and Joe Bing. Now we see Joe, recruiting such help in the capitol, and slated for Sarkhan himself. This meeting also affords an excellent example of description, one of three techniques

indispensible to narrative writing. The father and uncle roles are particularly fitting to Dartmouth's Upton and Northwestern's Bing.

Again we see mediocrity honored as the norm. Bing's sales talk is not a challenge to talent but a sudden, unexpected opportunity for easy life, opening before the unsuccessful. No hardships will be experienced, nor will preparation be required. One will not even be expected to learn the language since interpreters are cheap - as well as a favorite role for spies. We do not need Upton's sour summation to drive the authors' point home. And even Hamilton is consistent. He expresses pessimism about Atkins, a lone source of what should have been consolation to a recruiter of foreign help.

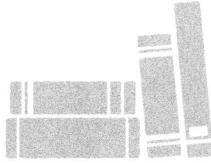

THE UGLY AMERICAN

CHAPTER SEVEN

. . . .

THE GIRL WHO GOT RECRUITED

To Marie Macintosh, member of Upton's audience in the last chapter, the acceptance of her application for duty overseas means escape from buses, cafeterias and unbroken evenings of T.V. in a crowded apartment.

She writes her ex-roommates a month later telling of her paid - for first-class flight and reception by a chauffeur-driven car. She tells of a house and staff of servants to make dinner for ten an easy matter. Marie stresses the low cost of everything for Government employees, and reveals that she has bought a Hillman, duty-free and with no transportation cost. For the first time in her life she can save money, due to the increase in pay granted at Sarkhan, a hardship post.

Comment: Sears' letter home was a gem. Marie's is a masterpiece. Nothing could picture more clearly,

between the lines, our stupidity in Far Eastern foreign policy. On this mediocre and totally unqualified girl money has been spent in amounts which become alarming when magnified by many like her. She has been given a free flight and virtually been presented with a car. She lives in a state of comparative luxury unimagined in her drab Washington existence. Unable to speak one word in Sarkhanese, she will never meet a native or do anything to improve our position abroad. Yet she is extended rates at government stores so generous that she can hardly believe them. Father Finian could not get ball point pens to help circulate a paper which was defeating Communism. But Marie MacIntosh is saving money, partly, of course, because Sarkhan is a hardship post.

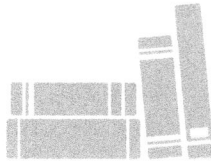

THE UGLY AMERICAN

CHAPTER EIGHT

. . . .

THE AMBASSADOR AND THE WORKING PRESS

Ambassador Sears stuns Asian journalists and infuriates their American colleague when he refuses to comment on a story printed in an anti-American Sarkhanese newspaper. The article alleges that the Sarkhanese Air Force is going to be evicted from their American-owned base because past Sarkhanese expenditures there have made that once useless property a profitable buy for American speculators. Privately, Sears reveals that he doesn't know whether the story is a lie or not. Then he prepares happily for his departure and awaiting federal judgeship before the arrival of his successor, Gilbert MacWhite.

Comment: It is beginning to look more like a novel. Finian is active enough here in Sarkhan to be refused protection. And Colvin's return is blocked only by a lame-duck Ambassador. As yet, there is no protagonist. But if the plot is to be a struggle

for Sarkhan between the United States and Russia, Sears' exit leaves an important role open. Who is MacWhite? Will he be another unwilling incompetent like Sears? Or will he resemble one of those unofficial Americans interested enough in his job to prepare for it? How will he react to Bing, Colvin and Finian? Under his ambassadorship, will Finian encounter Krupitzyn on even terms? And will Lucky Lou #2 have an answer to the trained Jesuit tactics before which Vinich fell? Not since Colvin was dropped so suddenly have we looked ahead with such a normal novel-reader's interest to the next chapter.

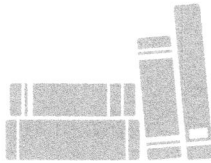

THE UGLY AMERICAN

CHAPTER NINE

. . . .

EVERYONE HAS EARS

Gilbert MacWhite is as good an ambassador as Sears was a bad one. Nevertheless, he makes a serious mistake upon his arrival in Sarkhan. Because he likes two elderly Chinese servants at the American Embassy, and because his own traps have failed to reveal any knowledge of English on their part, he trusts them. It takes his friend, Li Pang, a representative of Chiang Kai-shek, to expose these Chinese as involuntary Communist spies.

His mistake convinces MacWhite he doesn't know enough about Asians and their deadly finality in the game of politics. He is also convinced he can learn from travel and observation. He secures permission to visit the Philippines and Viet Nam.

Comment: Two basic weaknesses of American foreign service are the theme of this chapter.

First, even the best qualified American diplomat possesses a comparative naivete which is dangerous in Asian politics. There, they play "for keeps." MacWhite admires the many genuine good traits of the two Chinese servants, Donald and Roger. He has failed to catch them in his own traps. Therefore they must be trustworthy. Two things apparently never occurred to him. One was that the most admirable person might be forced into espionage. The other was that his own traps were not a final test. MacWhite would have genuinely denied that he was either naive or egotistical. It is a shock when he realizes that he has been both.

The second inherent flaw in our foreign service is the almost one hundred percent employment of native servants. This one has already been noted by MacWhite. Nevertheless, it becomes his downfall.

A comparison of two excellent representatives of their respective countries accentuates these flaws. Both MacWhite and Krupitzyn are intelligent, able men. Each has made every preparation for his ambassadorial post. But MacWhite has never seen his parents murdered, and then been trained to look upon their killer as a new parent. Naivete has little place in such a world. Neither did Gilbert bring with him to Sarkhan a domestic staff completely filled with dedicated American replicas of his younger self, learning their careers as they work.

Detailed description is employed here, as in the first chapter, to enhance the deadliness and savagery of a scene. Li's icy eyes, the white mark around his nose and mouth and the tensing of his body which causes Donald's instinctive recoil are all examples. So, too, are the four red marks left on Donald's cheek and the detailed description of third degree meted out by Sarkhanese police. But here also, as in the first chapter, shock effects are used only as the story demands them.

THE UGLY AMERICAN

CHAPTER TEN

· ·

THE RAGTIME KID

Colonel Hillandale, United States Air Force, has three loves: jazz, food, and every kind of people. The Ragtime Kid soon becomes unofficial advisor to Ramon Magsaysay. He campaigns for Magsaysay in a Presidential campaign. Visiting a Northern province where Communists have identified Magsaysay as a friend of wealthy, snobbish Americans, Hillandale convinces them that he is one American who is neither snobbish nor rich. Magsaysay carries the province.

Comment: The scene has shifted but the theme is the same. Americans in their natural state make good ambassadors. It is only when official and unnatural that they do not. Unfortunately, the last two words too often go together. MacWhite is an exception. So too was Ruth Jyoti's friend, Bob

Maile in Setkya. But Sears and Joe Bing are not. Hillandale now joins Colvin and Father Finian as a natural ambassador. Their popularity with the natives is much greater than the dislike shown them by the official representatives of the country they are serving so effectively. And they continue to serve it despite opposition from its State Department.

THE UGLY AMERICAN

CHAPTER ELEVEN

· ·

THE IRON OF WAR

Major James (Tex) Wolchek, a veteran of two wars reports as an observer to French Major Monet in Viet Nam. Tex volunteers for action again although he obeys the rules governing observation.

Tex can no more understand the defeats suffered by expertly led, fearless French troops than can Monet himself. Neither can visiting ambassador MacWhite, who brings news of the defeat at Dien Bien Phu. The American observing officer suggests that the answer may lie in the military writings of Mao Tse-tung. Unconvinced at first, Monet changes his mind when Jim Davis and another soldier return, horribly tortured, from patrol duty.

Comment: The book of rules has been questioned! Readers of Marquand's Melville Goodwin, USA, can appreciate the sacrilege of Tex's suggestion where a professional service man like Monet was involved.

True, this book, in which all answers lie, was held up to ridicule by Herman Wouk in The Caine Mutiny. The criticism was justified here, however, only because of petty interpretation by the incompetent Captain Queeg. As soon as the dry, able Captain White took charge, the book and the service were restored.

The scene has been shifted for the posing of this latest challenge by the authors in a swiftly paced, savagely interesting drama. Unprepared, mediocre, official America is no longer being outwitted by its superbly readied and competent Russian counterpart in Sarkhan. This time it is France which is falling before Communism in Viet Nam. Nor is the cast the same. No type such as Louis Sears or Joe Bing is to be found among the fearlessly fighting Legionnaires, ably led by their officers. The fault lies only in the French High Command which, like its American counterpart in the State Department, has refused to study the enemy as the latter is always willing to study it.

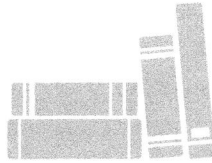

THE UGLY AMERICAN

CHAPTER TWELVE

THE LESSONS OF WAR

Tex, Monet, and MacWhite learn from Mao's book that guerrilla fighting must be centered around a command post within half an hour's march of their battle site. Locating such a post, they destroy it in a night attack, and then retreat from the scene of their first victory.

Before an audience of generals gathered through MacWhite's influence, the three report their success. The only reaction is angry disbelief coupled with outrage at the suggestion that modern chiefs of staff could learn anything from Chinese guerrillas. Soon after, the French evacuate Hanoi. Their conquerors enter, mostly on foot, looking like an army of three hundred years ago. But they have won.

Comment: Neither American Wolchek nor French Monet should have been surprised. The military high

command in their countries has the habit of refusing to recognize either new ideas or talent. Mitchell was rebuked for suggesting that the Air Force could be a major factor in warfare, and De Gaulle's ideas of lightning war were ridiculed until the Germans used them against his countrymen. The Union Chiefs of Staff took half the Civil War to discover the man destined to lead them to victory. And the Supreme Commander in World War II spent an incredible number of years as aide in the Philippines. This chapter, like the last, implants deeper in our perception the fatal flaws in policy which is costing the West victory in Asia, and threatening it with ultimate defeat there. It is also teaching, through absorbing narration, how easily the situation could be reversed if those capable of victory did not have to fight their superiors as well as the enemy.

THE UGLY AMERICAN

CHAPTER THIRTEEN

. . . .

WHAT WOULD YOU DO IF YOU WERE PRESIDENT?

At a dinner in Burma, journalist U Maung Swe tries to account for loss of American prestige in southeastern Asia. He attributes it to the general obnoxiousness of most Americans abroad. Also, our aid is generally coupled with conditions which cause Asians to lose face.

Russian aid, while not better, is, in his opinion, more effective as propaganda because it is based upon a greater understanding of Asian needs.

Speaking privately with MacWhite later, U tells him that Colvin was framed, and suggests his return.

Comment: For once these authors forget that their primary function is to entertain, not to teach. The whole chapter is not only uninteresting but also

unconvincing. Ruth Jyoti was vividly drawn, even though she was primarily a figure voicing the authors' views, but here everything is unreal. The questions sound contrived and the answers are uninspired repetitions of truths hitherto brought out in gripping narration. For once the reader is told how to think. This is a cardinal sin in good fiction.

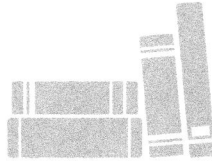

THE UGLY AMERICAN

. . . .

HOW TO BUY AN AMERICAN JUNIOR GRADE

Tom Knox, American agricultural expert, is immensely popular in Cambodian villages where the natives consider him a miracle-worker among the chickens. Also, he has always wanted to see the world.

This desire proves to be Tom's Achilles heel. Angered by official refusal to adopt his suggestions for improving native chickens, Tom resigns, announcing that he is going home to plead his case before Congress. With subtle flattery, the French and rich Cambodians arrange a tour home for him through the wonder spots of Asia and Europe. His anger is lulled into oblivion, and no letters are ever written to Congress.

Comment: French diplomats may not understand native Asians, but they certainly know how to influence Americans from the Middle West. Even

Krupitzyn might have taken a lesson from them before visiting the Chief Abbot. They detect weakness and dispel suspicion with a subtlety which Louis could only have hoped to emulate, not surpass. And in lulling anger into oblivion, they employ the hospitality and charm for which they have become legendary. Here is a propaganda program based upon understanding, sophisticated flattery, and tact such as has never been seen in official Westerners in the Far East. In it the French are aided by the type of Asians whose wealth might have won a nod even from Joe Bing in his cafe at the Hotel Montaigne. The tragic implication of such misplaced talent constitutes that artistic revelation of truth necessary to good fiction. It is far more effective here than in the last chapter.

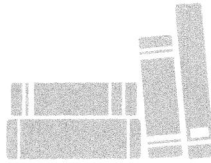

THE UGLY AMERICAN

CHAPTER FIFTEEN

....

THE SIX-FOOT SWAMI FROM SAVANNAH

In Sarkhan, Colonel Hillandale notices the number and respectability of fortune-tellers, and realizes that his own hobby, palm reading, may be useful.

In a private reading for the Prime Minister at a dinner, he makes a deep impression with researched knowledge of the past and predictions of the future, based upon wide-awake observations by Hillandale during his tour of the capital. The Prime Minister wishes to arrange an appointment for Hillandale to read the King's palm.

Hillandale is sure he can help the American cause with a successful reading. But George Swift, charge d'affaires, doesn't think the matter worth following through and bungles the arrangements.

Comment: The writing in this book has been realistic up until now, but here the reader's credulity begins to be strained. Not by the power of palm reading, for its dignity and popularity in the country have been made convincingly clear. Rather it is by the ease with which an outsider picks up classified information. It is hardly probable that information connected with the Ambassador's past lay in the public files. Or even information about the charge d'affaires. Yet the reader must assume this. Certainly nothing which happened here could have happened without this being the case. Also, Hillandale's plan to impress the King was based upon a calculated use of gossip picked up from domestics. Certainly, after the episode of Donald in the chapter "Everyone Has Ears," we have difficulty in believing that knowledge not guarded from servants in an Asian palace would be considered detectable only by the occult.

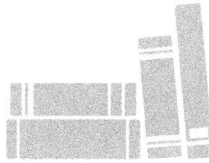

THE UGLY AMERICAN

CHAPTER SIXTEEN

. . . .

CAPTAIN BONING, U S N

Solomon Asch, head of the special Armament Section to the Asia Conference, realizes his biggest obstacle lies in Asian sensitivity. He feels sure that none of his delegates will deliberately affront the Asians by overt superior conduct. He warns his delegates against too much social life, knowing they must be alert for all questions. Nevertheless, Captain Boning, naval officer and armaments expert, allows himself to be absorbed in off hours by a Chinese lady, Dr. Ruby Tsung, who has been secretly educated in the Soviet Union. Exhausted, he misses a question, antagonizes the Asians, and America's goal of gaining Burman and Indian permission for installing weapons within their boundaries fails.

> **Comment: It might have happened to anybody, but its deadly effect was due to original diplomatic stupidity. The United States is not the complete villain in this chapter, although the immediate victim is an**

American. Indeed, Asch's open opposition comes from the French and English. He can take care of their suggestions of a superior attitude. He does this by first admitting their greater experience, and then describing in graphic New Yorkese exactly where it has led them. This act will mean two more critical reports on him, but he merely adds them mentally to a pile he is sure Ambassador Dooling has started. It is not any of these, however, but Anderson, the political expert, who started the ball rolling toward defeat. If anyone should have known about Ruby's Communistic connections, it would have been he. Nevertheless, it is Anderson who introduces her to Boning.

However, it is not his mistake or Boning's susceptibility which makes this incident fit into the pattern of the book. Rather it is the background of a Western policy of superiority to Asians which make the Captain's subsequent weakness fatal. Spies have outwitted other people before, but their work has seldom been so easy for them by years of blunder. Ruby did not have to elicit information from her victim. She merely needed to produce one moment of incompetence - and all results of former Western errors went to work for her side.

TEXTUAL ANALYSIS

CHAPTER SEVENTEEN

· ·

THE UGLY AMERICAN

Homer Atkins, ugly and retired millionaire engineer, is as disgusted with bureaucrats in Viet Nam as he has been with them all his life. Invited here to advise on dam and military highway construction, he has toured the country, and then advised on smaller constructions for civilian agricultural needs in the backcountry. Everybody becomes angry, and Homer quits. However, visiting Ambassador MacWhite interests him in the irrigation problems of Sarkhan, and leaves Atkins seated at a cafe table absorbed in his sketch of a pump which may solve the problem.

> **Comment: A problem rises here, the question of clarity. With the vaguest of information given, we can only guess as to the contents of Homer's report. We are equally uncertain as to the cause of the anger which pervades this chapter from the beginning. Had Atkins changed his whole assignment in that**

report? From the beginning, had he told employers, awaiting reports on highways, how he was going to build brick factories instead? And did he expect them to remain silent, and to act only when they found those factories good or bad? If so, his anger at their questions could certainly be called naive. Or, called upon to explain surveys of military highways never located, had he given his explanations at the conference before we were permitted to sit in? Was he angered because they, unlike MacWhite, did not want to listen?

None of this, however, detracts from the fine use of description and scene employed throughout the chapter. We can see Atkins, and, by contrast, the supercilious representatives of Viet Nam and France. And the scene at the cafe is a vivid picture of an absorbed, creative artist being observed by an Ambassador deepened in his judgment of men through experience. Also, there is no obscurity connected with the main objective here.

Again, the writers make us see that lack of understanding of native needs which characterizes Western policy in Asia. We also see added to it a greed and exploitation which has led Asians to expect the worst. We already have seen an example of its effect in Chapter Two. There, it made Krupitzyn's task of stealing credit for the rice a comparatively simple one.

THE UGLY AMERICAN

CHAPTER EIGHTEEN

. . . .

THE UGLY AMERICAN AND THE UGLY SARKHANESE

In Sarkhan, Homer Arkins seeks to replace handbucket irrigation with a native mechanized system. Workable and cheap piping and mechanism are attained with bamboo pipes and discarded jeep parts. His wife, Emma suggests the drive mechanism of a discarded bicycle for cheap powering.

Jeepo, a native mechanic, almost as homely and able as Homer, helps make such a pump work; but then tells Atkins bluntly that bicycles are too valuable to be discarded in Sarkhan until useless even for such a pump. Jeepo suggests using the rear wheel of a good bicycle as a treadmill. The machine can still be employed for transportation. Homer and he become business partners.

Comment: Once more the redeeming unofficial side of the picture is painted. Atkins takes his place with

Colvin and Father Finian as Americans who want to help natives help themselves. Unlike diplomats described by journalist U Maung Swe, Atkins is always conscious of face, and the necessity of preserving face to both for himself and the Sarkhanese. Never does he appear the rich, powerful, favor-bestowing representative of the West. The pump is a mutual creation of his and Jeepo's. If he demands a share of the profits, it is only because all know that he is just as smart and industrious as his partner.

Have we discovered the hero? Is Homer the Ugly American for whom this book is named? Had he appeared earlier, we might have thought so. Unfortunately, his entry has been too long delayed, and "ugly" will have an uglier interpretation than that of mere homeliness.

THE UGLY AMERICAN

CHAPTER NINETEEN

....

THE BENT BACKS OF CHANG' DONG

Emma Atkins, as plain as her engineer husband, Homer, is ugly, connects the bent elderly backs in the Sarkhanese village, Chang 'Dong, with the fact that only older people sweep, and always with short-handled brooms.

Knowing that imported long broom handles will never break a native custom and equally aware that local wood is too valuable for sweeping, Emma solves the problem by finding a grove of long reeds like the short ones now used for handles. She makes a handle of proper length and then lets amazed natives notice her erect posture while sweeping. Told of the grove, they depart to gather their own handles; and later build a shrine which will be in memory of Emma.

Comment: Americans are the best ambassadors - when they act like Americans. Ugly, efficient, and

generous, Homer and Emma Atkins prove this. They behave with a kindness and tact which Asians have admired in America, but never see in official Americans abroad. And the couple help Asians to help themselves.

This chapter is also an excellent example of the fine kind of fiction described by Harold C. Gardiner in *Norms for the Novel*. It is a blend of truth and beauty which instructs even as it entertains. We do not go to this book to learn how people should treat one another, nor to discover how they react when such treatment is received. Nevertheless, we find out, as we identify ourselves easily with these characters in an artistically described natural situation.

THE UGLY AMERICAN

CHAPTER TWENTY

. . . .

SENATOR, SIR...

Senator Brown, skilled and tough interrogator, has come to Viet Nam to find justification for enormous American expenditures - or lack of it. But the French and Americans who are to be investigated exploit his age, arthritic legs, and heart condition. They make his trip as physically difficult as possible. Besides, he doesn't speak Vietnamese - and his interpreter has been briefed. He rarely meets subordinates. As a result, he finds himself accepting all the French high command reasons for defeat even as he is horrified by films of Communist brutalities.

Back home on the Senate floor, he discredits the true report of Ambassador MacWhite which is being presented by another Senator.

Comment: In Chapter Fourteen, we have learned "How to Buy an American Junior Grade." Here we

learn how to handle an American Senator. In both cases we have the implication of misplaced talent. Apparently the Embassy makes no effort to keep its people working to influence Asians in favor of the United States. On the other hand, it spares no efforts to keep them on their toes when the objective is to deceive Washington. All the actions condoned while they were antagonizing the natives are now vetoed. Cars, cocktail parties, cafes, and plain slacking are out for the duration of Brown's visit.

Also, as in the case of Tom Brown, personal weaknesses are noted and evaluated for unofficial aims, as they never are in considering official work. A crowning irony here is the exploitation of the visitor's ignorance of the native language by Embassy officials, exactly as it has so often been exploited against them.

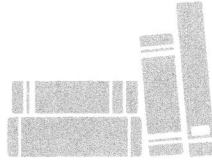

THE UGLY AMERICAN

CHAPTER TWENTY-ONE

· ·

THE SUM OF TINY THINGS

After Senator Brown's attack, Ambassador MacWhite receives an informal letter from his friend, the Secretary of State, saying that he has been disturbed by MacWhite's opinions expressed in countries where he had no official status.

MacWhite's answer is a list of conditions for future employment in foreign service accompanied by an offer of resignation. These conditions include abolishment of commissaries and PX's, no dependents for service under two years, some knowledge of Sarkhanese, and the reading of leading Communist writers.

The Secretary accepts MacWhite's resignation, and implies that his successor will be Joe Bing.

Comment: The authors sum up in MacWhite's last letter. They warn that without change in our foreign policy, we cannot win in southeastern Asia short of starting a nuclear war ourselves. Our present struggle is being lost in countless little ways in little incidents. We will continue to lose here and eventually, everywhere, unless we replace the incompetent and unqualified with dedicated and prepared people in foreign service.

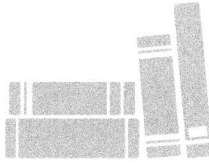

THE UGLY AMERICAN

CHAPTER TWENTY-TWO

. . . .

A FACTUAL EPILOGUE

This chapter justifies the truths presented in fiction in this book. Incompetence, mediocrity and unpreparedness as exemplified in incidents described here have been witnessed by these authors. Asia, itself, like Deong, is a former American friend now turned Communist.

Recruiting geared to mediocrity is not actually mythical. Until the Finians, Colvins, Hillandales, Atkinses and Wolcheks appear within our official ranks, we will never be respected as a nation, as we are as people, for our inherent principles which we fail too often to recognize in foreigners.

Comment: In this chapter the authors speak directly to give information. No longer is it their purpose first to entertain and then to teach, if possible. We are told directly that Communists got to Asia, our former

friend, and that we did not. Neither do we learn the impracticability of our grandiose plans in Asia as spectators at a conference while we watch Homer's anger rise. We are told bluntly how stupid it is to build motor highways in a country where everyone walks. This epilogue is an interesting summation of what the authors have presented as education in the guise of entertainment.

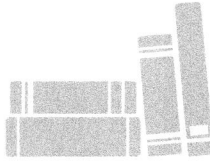

THE UGLY AMERICAN

LOUIS SEARS

American Ambassador to Sarkhan, may not be the Ugly American of the title, but his character and actions as our representative abroad would certainly qualify him. He is an opportunist who doesn't want to bother working at whatever job he has; he sees every event only as a chance to advance his personal well-being. He has shrewdness, an eye out for the main chance, but not the intelligence or the desire to build himself, through his opportunities, to a really worthwhile post of responsibility. Above all, he has no conception of his obligation to the country - the United States - that is supporting him, or the country - Sarkhan - whose goodwill he is supposed to be cultivating.

JOHN COLVIN

An American of goodwill and initiative. He also has a certain amount of naivete; he thinks he can by-pass the red tape of officialdom and give help directly to the Sarkhanese. He has had the capacity to learn, an invaluable trait in anyone dealing with nationals of another country; he has learned many good things from the Sarkhanese. With his direct nature, he thinks the way to do a thing is to go ahead and do it. He has to learn cunning and the art of self-preservation from a Sarkhanese turned Communist; here Colvin may be a symbol of what American diplomacy may have to learn.

DEONG

Another example of an opportunist. Deong doesn't really believe in anything: his Communism is not a matter of conviction but of getting on what he believes is the winning team. Like Sears, he shows shrewdness, not the kind of intelligence which wants to figure things out for itself. He has none of the feelings we commonly associate with cultured humanity; he has no gratitude for what Colvin had done for him, he has no compassion for the humans who will get in the way of his self-preservation. He is almost the Sarkhanese opposite number of Sears.

LOUIS KRUPTZYN

The Soviet Union's Ambassador to Sarkhan typifies what we have to learn from the Russian strategy. He, too, is shrewd and opportunistic, but he has the intelligence to apply himself wholeheartedly to his job. He is under no illusions, as is the American Ambassador, that his mere presence in Sarkhan is sufficient. He is out to impress the Sarkhanese with the Soviet way of life, and he understands that the first way to impress anyone - individual or nation - is to understand that very way of life he is going to try to change. In short, he is prepared on all counts; both to understand another's way of life and to take every opportunity of impressing his own way of life on others. He is also intelligent enough never to underestimate an enemy, as exemplified by his concern over Father Finian.

FATHER FINIAN

An example of a dedicated, trained man. He has known the strict discipline of the Jesuits; he knows that to do a job, he must give himself over wholly to the conditions of the job. He immerses himself in Burmese life, enduring great physical discomfort with the stoicism of a soldier (which he considers himself to be, since he is fighting for his beliefs) and overcomes suspicion of the white man in the only effective way: making himself one with the Burmese. He is an example of the power of disciplined, directed belief.

RUTH JYOTI

A clear-eyed Eurasian. She is not so much a character as a spokesman for every American who has been in Asia and been disgusted with those who are bungling our position abroad.

JOE BING

He epitomizes one of the worst types of Americans abroad. He has neither real intelligence nor shrewdness, just a sort of animal satisfaction with himself and his material advantages. His bluff heartiness is a mask for an empty, smug mind. Because of his official position, he is a positive danger to America.

BOB MAILE

An exceptional USIS official, he has a conscience and a sense of obligation to his job. He is completely unpretentious, never trying to impress anyone with his importance. This latter trait, coupled with his intelligence in getting to know the language and the people of the country in which he was working, make him one of our really effective ambassadors abroad.

MARIE MACINTOSH

She is not really a character, but a stereotype of the average lower-echelon employee sent abroad by the State Department. She is completely without training, qualifications or special ability, nor does she show any particular desire to put in her time abroad profitably, by learning about her hosts or sharing with them any of the advantages of her country.

GILBERT MACWHITE

Sears' successor as American Ambassador to Sarkhan, he is cut of an entirely different cloth. He is intelligent, able, trained, and anxious to do an effective job. He is confident of his abilities, and prides himself on having a certain amount of sophistication in matters of the diplomatic life. When the incident of the two Chinese servants shows him how much he has to learn, he accepts his lesson and sets out to learn what he needs to. In fact, his ability to learn, to expose himself to new knowledge and to evaluate it, is what would have made him a peer among ambassadors -but, of course, lesser men can't stand such superior intelligence.

LI PANG

On the surface, a counterpart of MacWhite; cultured, intelligent, etc. He has another dimension, particularly Asiatic; an ability to smell out and uncover treachery. He symbolizes the lessons the MacWhites have to learn if they are to be effective in Asia.

DONALD AND ROGER

These two Chinese servants symbolize the unwilling service many people are trapped into by the Communists.

EDWIN B. HILLANDALE

The United States Air Force Colonel has the wit to disguise his hearty, well-fed and prosperous American self to win the favor of the Asians. He has the wit to assess the value of palm reading and astrology to the Asians, and the intelligence to follow through on this knowledge. In short, he knows that the key to nations is through the character and beliefs of their own people.

MAJOR JAMES (TEX) WOLCHEK

An American Major assigned as Observer with the Second Regiment Amphibie, Legion Etrangere, Tex has learned all he knows about war on active service with the Army. Because he has only direct experience and no background of tradition, he is willing to learn fresh ideas. He learns them in Viet Nam. He is able to appreciate that the French are being defeated because they are still following their old book of rules, while the Communists are following the new tactics outlined by Mao Tse-tung. He exemplifies the fresh American fighting force which came in to help the French in Viet Nam, and was still open to new lessons.

MAJOR MONET

Contrary to Tex, he is in the French military tradition. He cannot conceive, at first, that the French are wrong in the way they are fighting. He exemplifies French stubbornness in clinging to their traditions and way of doing things, even while it was costing them every advantage they had in Viet Nam.

TOM KNOX

A lovable, naive, goodhearted American, truly wanting to help the Asians, but without the guile to see through the French and Asian soft-soap which was applied to make him forget his justified anger. He is an example of what can be done by corrupt men when they want to manipulate someone who hasn't their guile.

GEORGE SWIFT

One of the very worst types of American officials abroad. He is gross and vulgar in his outlook. He is incapable of acknowledging that any way of life but his own exists. He is concerned only with impressing his superiors, and that only because he looks for promotions and better berths for George Swift. He is not above undermining other people to ensure his own security. He cares nothing whatever for the people among whom he is stationed.

SOLOMON ASCH

Head of the American Delegation to the Special Armament section of the Asia Conference, he is honest, realistic, and hard-boiled enough to see a difficult job through to the very end. That he fails is due to the cleverness of the Communists. He is, once again, a warning that even when every loophole has been plugged, each must be constantly checked for insidious attacks by the enemy.

CAPTAIN BONING

He is the weak link that undoes the strong chain Asch has built up. He falls into the oldest trap of all, a clever woman's manipulations of his interests. He symbolizes the fact that in any kind of war, including diplomatic, there is no room for even momentary lapses.

DOCTOR RUBY TSUNG

She represents a willing partner in the Soviet game of undermining the enemy. Her education, her training, her life, are devoted to working for Soviet interests, and she lets no personal likes or dislikes stand in her way. Her feelings are not her own; they are the State's.

HOMER ATKINS

An ugly American outwardly, he symbolizes more of what we need in other countries: intelligence, ability, practicality, humaneness. He might also symbolize what we look like to these people: ugly (for some reason the average American tourist puts his worst foot forward when abroad, with bad manners, loud voices, overdressing, arrogance, lack of appreciation of what he sees) but immensely rich. Underneath are all of Homer's good qualities. He is ingenious, and he is quick-witted in dealing with people, knowing how to take the Asians on their own terms.

JEEPO

The Sarkhanese mechanic might be considered ugly because he doesn't conform to the standard picture of the passive,

67

smooth Oriental who doesn't understand American ways. He understands them very well, knows how to use them for his own ends, and is quick, deft and able in his handling of mechanical things, which is supposedly an exclusively American trait.

EMMA ATKINS

In a sense, she is typical of what an American woman might be able to do for Asian women. She has the frontier spirit; she is resourceful, she is quietly clever, she knows how to teach by precept, not preaching. It is not surprising that the natives build a shrine to her, for her qualities might be goddess-like to a people who live by tradition, and have been taught by her to find new ways.

JONATHAN BROWN

The Senator might well typify many of our politicians. The means he used to get to the top were questionable, to say the least; but once there, he became a solid asset to the country. However, with all his good intentions, his new-found incorruptibility and his intelligence, he has not the extra dimension needed: the skepticism of what he sees on the surface that would make him probe deeper, make a little extra effort, question the motives of those with whom he was mingling, to come up with the true facts. Like many Congressmen who have spent little time abroad, he too willingly discredits the solid knowledge of a man like MacWhite. It might not be too much to say that such "good" men as Senator Jonathan Brown are as much responsible for our present foreign-relations difficulties as are such villains as Sears and Swift.

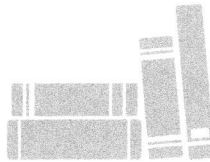

THE UGLY AMERICAN

. . . .

Why Not A Novel? *The Ugly American* cannot be called a novel, but its writers were more than story tellers. The reader asks, "And then?" but he also asks, "Why?". Lederer and Burdick have produced a work which challenges intelligence and memory as much as it does curiosity.

This book is as provocative as it is interesting. We cannot imagine an uninformed incompetent such as Sears lasting more than a week as executive in a profit-and-loss business. Yet in southeastern Asia, where our investments to retain Communism have been staggering, we see them protected by one whom the enemy cherishes as a jewel, and whose mistakes, they insist, must continue. It is a bitter commentary on American ineptitude in foreign relations.

There are many reasons for disqualifying it as a novel. It has no plot, no **protagonist**, and no orderly ending in the plot sense. No character has been caught up in a chain of events within or without his control, and has developed or been destroyed as the planned action works towards a climax. Nor do the characters have to interact and subordinate themselves as they contribute to such action. For the most part, they work side by side but not together, in the same locality.

Why Not A Collection Of Short Stories? Neither is it a collection of short stories, as it was once described in *The New York Times*. Too many of the chapters lack that orderly series of incidents all arranged in a graded ascent to a single predominating one; although often they do produce that singleness of effect demanded of the short story. Four exceptions here which might be short stories in themselves are "Nine Friends," "How to Buy an American Junior Grade," "Captain Boning, USN," and "The Bent Backs of Chang 'Dong." For the most part, however, the chapters resemble installments in a serial. We hurry to the next to learn whether Colvin can remain, or Krupitzyn can resist Finian; and too often we don't find out.

What Then? If not short story writers or novelists, then perhaps the writers can be called prophets in literature. Certainly, their book does not resemble a picture of combat between good and evil, such as that presented by Melville in *Moby Dick*. And yet there is sometimes seen in their work that quality of extension which characterizes prophetic writing. Colvin and the Atkins couple are not just helpful people in isolated southeastern Asian communities. They are also examples of the truly understanding and sensible friends found everywhere throughout time. If not a novel, *The Ugly American* certainly carries an angry and ominous message.

Indeed, if we look upon the characters as symbols rather than people, and discard momentarily the arbitrary demand that the novel must be a plotted story of individuals, this work does resemble that literary form.

Then, there is a chain of events leading up to the climactic failure of talent in Sarkhan. That mythical country itself becomes the prize in a struggle between International Communism and American Intervention, both trying to win Nationalism as their ally. And the struggle there is symbolic of the same real one throughout southeastern Asia. Anecdotes or separate short stories laid in Burma, the Philippines, or Viet Nam no longer become diversions breaking the continuity, but may be regarded as subplots contributing to the central **theme**. *The Ugly American* may be taken as a composite of many inferior characters, and the manner in which he, in countless little ways, is contributing to our downfall in the Far East. Indeed, the great international struggle is only a background to the one pictured here. This book portrays, more than anything else, the truly internal national struggle between the talented, devoted, and prepared unofficial few and the vast majority of incompetent and mediocre officials, utterly lacking in either preparation or ambition. MacWhite's dismissal and Bing's succession constitute a fitting **climax** to what, looked at in this way, is an angry novel with a message of disaster.

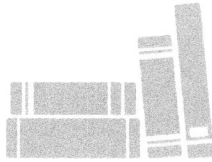

THE UGLY AMERICAN

. . . .

Question: Discuss Gilbert MacWhite as a possible hero of *The Ugly American.*

Answer: There are arguments for and against MacWhite as a candidate for the hero's role in *The Ugly American.* In the affirmative, he appears more or less consistently in at least two-thirds of the story. This is far more than can be said of any other single character in the book. He also is the only character who can claim principal participation in a logical chain of events leading up to a **climax**. A true exponent of America's containment policy, MacWhite is determined to defeat Communism in Sarkhan during his ambassadorship. Possessing a natural aptitude for foreign service, he has had the benefit of long and hard training in that field. Also, he has prepared for this post with a thoroughness that would have won approval from dedicated missionary or modern Muscovite. And he begins his plan of campaign immediately upon assuming office.

A third argument in MacWhite's favor is the way his character develops as he reacts to the different situations in which he is placed. Set back in devastating fashion when his naivete utterly ruins the opening step in his campaign, he turns this experience into a lesson rather than a permanently disabling injury. Taking all blame, he becomes convinced he has much to learn about the deadly arena of Asian diplomacy. Accordingly he asks and receives permission to travel. His resulting growth and improved ability to size up men and situations are seen in subsequent encounters with Wolchek, Monet and Atkins.

Finally, MacWhite is the victim in the **climax** of this story when his dismissal and Bing's succession mark a defeat of talent and triumph of mediocrity in American foreign service.

Against MacWhite's candidacy for the role of hero is the fact that his casting would render the title of this book meaningless. There is nothing ugly about MacWhite. Distinguished, fit, controlled, and tactful, he cannot possibly qualify for this adjective.

Also, too often, his appearances are last-minute and have the semblance of being contrived. This is especially true in the chapter "What Would You Do If You Were President?" and "The Ugly American." Again, it is hardly believable that the first news of defeat at Dien Bien Phu would be brought to French troops preparing to drop there by a visiting American Ambassador.

Question: How had colonialism created obstacles for Father Finian and Homer Atkins?

Answer: The legacy of colonialism, in Burma as in Sarkhan, was one of inferiority and suspicion. Both had to be overcome by Father Finian, but only the second by Homer Atkins.

In Finian's case the price was greater because the degree of loyalty and trust required was greater in a matter involving life and death. Finian had one advantage. He was a Catholic dealing with Catholics and against a foe which was avowedly atheistic. Even so, colonialism had left so strong a feeling of racial inferiority due to second-class citizenship that Finian's Catholicism was more than outweighed by his white skin. As a Caucasian, he was denied their trust and allegiance until he could speak, eat and crouch like them. Then and only then could he, not as a white dictator, but as a fellow learner, plot with them in his campaign to destroy Communism.

Homer Atkins, on the other hand, had only to overcome distrust in a situation where the penalty of failure would be not his but that of the natives he was trying to help. Nevertheless, he could never have helped them with their irrigation problems by giving them the benefit of his skill, had he not first overcome the image of the white man eternally exploiting natives which generations of colonialism had implanted deeply in the village of Chang 'Dong. At every turn those villagers were waiting for the hitch in Homer's scheme which would show them they were being guiled again. Only after he had used native material, a native mechanic, native salesmen, and signed a contract, was this image of the duping Caucasian dispelled.

Question: What were three views of Communism described in this book?

Answer: Communism meant three different things to three characters in this book.

For the young marine encountered by Finian in his role as Navy Chaplain, Communism was a political religion worth dying for and above all argument. He would have been no more disturbed by proof of its illogic than would a Catholic have been shaken by revelation that the inquest was brutal.

To Deong, as to the child Louis Krupitzyn, it was the hand behind the gun, the inevitable winner, whose alliance had to be courted as quickly as possible. Justification for this point of view lay in the superior training and preparation of its representatives, as well as in the propaganda value of aid based upon an understanding of native needs. Also, this view was kept from being shattered by the always clever concealment, as far as the Deongs were concerned, of the ultimate destruction of the currently fostered nationalism by the eventual proletariat revolution.

To Father Finian, it was the face of the devil come on earth again to test men's souls. He recognized in it all those characteristics which had made conversion possible by the Church, with the one terrible difference: it was as devoted to evil as the Church was to good. In it he saw a rival faith that could not exist simultaneously with his own.

BIBLIOGRAPHY

WORKS BY LEDERER AND BURDICK

Lederer, William, *A Nation of Sheep* (New York, 1961). William Lederer, this time alone, attacks American official action abroad, particularly for its reluctance to give information.

Burdick, Eugene, *The 480* (New York, 1964). This time it is Eugene Burdick who attacks alone, and his target is the operation of the American political system in a Presidential campaign.

_____, *The Ninth Wave* (New York, 1956). This book by Eugene Burdick was called "one of the most realistic portraits of the American political scene...." by J. F. Sullivan in *Commonweal*.

Lederer, William and Burdick, Eugene, *Sarkhan* (New York, 1965). Seven years later, Lederer and Burdick collaborate again in a novel laid in the mythical Far Eastern country of *The Ugly American*. Their attack is more savage than before and with reason.

COLONIALISM, NATIONALISM, AND INTERVENTION

Hammer, Ellen Joy, *The Struggle for Indochina* (New York, 1954). A complete history of the rise of nationalism in Viet Nam under Ho Chi Minh in the north and, to a lesser extent, in the form of the Associated State in the south. Later espousal of Ho Chi Minh's Democratic Republic of Viet Nam by the Communists is also described in this book, as is the background of French colonialism against which the war in Indochina was fought.

Vo Nguyen Giap, *People's War, People's Army* (Prager, 1963). A Viet Cong insurrection manual for undeveloped countries. In it Ho Chi Minh's victorious general at Dien Bien Phu describes the tactics which bring success in guerrilla warfare. For political reasons, however, Giap could not admit that many of these tactics were first used and then described by Mao Tse-tung.

Parkinson, C. *Northcote, East and West* (Boston, 1963). This is a history of the alternate dominance of East and West since Sumerian days. A dismisser of world unity upon the grounds of resultant mental stagnation, Parkinson believes, nevertheless, that nuclear war potential necessitates the limiting of future conflicts to intellectual and cultural areas. He blames failure of the West today to its own lack of faith in anything.

THE UGLY AMERICAN AS A NOVEL

The Ugly American was first published in a hardbound edition by W. W. Norton & Company. It is also available in the paperbound Norton Library Edition and in the Fawcett paperbound edition.

Bently, Phyllis, *Some Observations On the Art of Narrative* (New York, 1947). The nature of three types of narrative: summary, scene and description, so ably employed by Lederer and Burdick, is clearly explained in this work.

Essenwein, J. B., *Writing the Short Story* (Cincinnati, 1918). In describing what a short story is not, Essenwein sets forth criteria for the novel.

Forster, E. M., *Aspects of the Novel* (New York, 1927). A series of lectures called the Clark Lectures and delivered under the auspices of Trinity College, Cambridge, constitutes this work. In them, Forster describes the prophetic type of writing with its element of extension which justifies the identification of *The Ugly American* as a novel.

Gardiner, Harold C., *Norms For the Novel* (New York, 1960). The element of beauty emerging in literature when truth of fact blends with truth of ideal as it does in "The Bent Backs of Chang 'Dong" is ably described in this work by Gardiner.

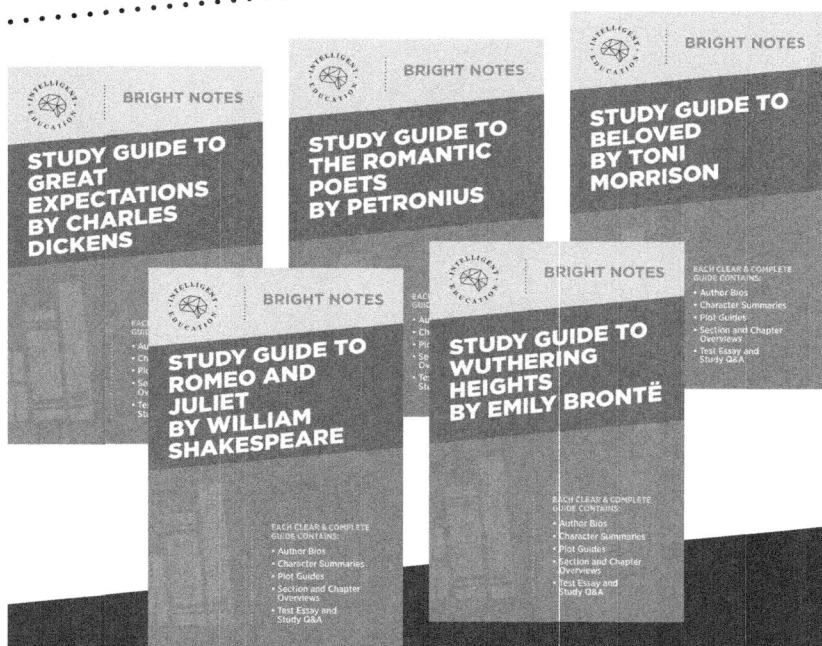

Printed by BoD in Norderstedt, Germany